PARALYMPIC POWER

Paul Mason

First published in 2019 by Wayland
Copyright © Hodder & Stoughton, 2019

Wayland
An imprint of
Hachette Children's Group
Part of Hodder and Stoughton
Carmelite House
50 Victoria Embankment
London EC4Y 0DZ

www.hachette.co.uk

Editor: Julia Bird
Design: RockJaw Creative

HB ISBN: 978 1 5263 0807 8
PB ISBN: 978 1 5263 0806 1

Printed in China

Please note: The statistics in this book were correct at the time of printing, but because of the nature of sport, it cannot be guaranteed that they are now accurate.

The words of the para athletes that appear in this book are taken from press interviews and other sources.

Picture credits: Aflo/REX/Shutterstock: 4, 26. Alhovik/Shutterstock: 8b. The Asahi Shimbun via Getty Images: 32t, 39. Lars Baron/Bongarts/Getty Images: 2, 34. Giorgio Benvenuri/EPA/REX/Shutterstock: 36r. Simon Bruty/OIS/IOC/AFP/Getty Images: 32b. Yasuyoshi Chiba/AFP/Getty Images: 16b, 23c, 29. Marco Ciccolella/Shutterstock: 40t. Gareth Copley/Getty Images: 7t. CP DC Press/Shutterstock: front cover 1, 10l, 12t. Raphael Dias/Getty Images: front cover r, 27. Harry Engels/Getty Images: 8tr. Darren England/EPA/REX/ Shutterstock: 45t. Julian Finney/Getty Images: 20. Focus Dzign/Shutterstock: 14. Kieran Galvin/NurPhoto/Getty Images: 25. Georgie Gillard/ANL/REX/Shutterstock: 33. ID1974/Shutterstock: 43. Kyodo News/Getty Images: 15c. Simon Lodge/OIS/IOC/AFP/Getty Images: 30. London News Pictures/REX/Shutterstock: 28. Thomas Lovelock for OIS/IOC/AFP/Getty Images: 8tl, 17. Bob Martin/OIS/IOC/AFP/Getty Images: 13l. Buda Mendes/Getty Images: 41. Aris Messinis/AFP/Getty Images: 45b. Andre Luiz Moreira/Shutterstock: 13r. Hannah Peters/Getty Images: 9b. Celso Pupo/Dreamstime: 12b. Andy Rain/EPA/REX/Shutterstock: 18. Lucy Ray/ANL/REX/Shutterstock: 37. Linnea Rheborg/Getty Images: 38, 40b. A. Ricardo/Shutterstock: 6, 7b, 22, 24c, 36l. Martin Rose/Bongarts/Getty Images: 42. Matthew Stockman/Getty Images: 1,11, 31. STR/AFP/Getty Images: 44. Bob Thomas/Getty Images: 5. Al Tielemans/OIS/IOC/AFP/Getty Images: 15bl. Atsushi Tomura/Getty Images: 21. Marek Trawczynski/Shutterstock: 9t. Lucas Uebel/Getty Images: front cover c. Friedmann Vogel/Getty Images: 19. Helene Wiesenhaan/Getty Images: 10r. Jamie Wiseman/ANL/REX/Shutterstock: 16c, 35. Andrew Wong/Getty Images: 24b. Xinhua/Alamy: 23b.

Every attempt has been made to clear copyright. Should there be any inadvertent omission please apply to the publisher for rectification.

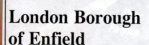

London Borough of Enfield		
91200000694236		
Askews & Holts	Mar-2020	
796.0456 JUNIOR NON-	£9.99	

CONTENTS

Paralympic power! ... 4

Paralympic classification ... 6

Archery ... 8

Shooting ... 9

Athletics ... 10

Triathlon ... 13

Badminton ... 14

Boccia ... 15

Canoeing ... 16

Rowing ... 17

Cycling ... 18

Football 5-a-side ... 20

Goalball ... 22

Judo ... 24

Taekwando ... 25

Powerlifting ... 26

Sitting volleyball ... 28

Wheelchair basketball ... 29

Swimming ... 30

Table tennis ... 34

Wheelchair tennis ... 35

Wheelchair fencing ... 36

Wheelchair rugby ... 37

Snowboard ... 38

Endurance skiing ... 40

Ice sports ... 42

Superstars extra ... 44

Glossary and Find out more ... 46

Index ... 48

PARALYMPIC POWER!

The Summer and Winter Paralympics happen every four years, soon after the Olympic Games. They are a chance for athletes with disabilities to compete at the highest level.

PARALYMPIC SPORTS
Many of the sports at the Games, such as some swimming and athletics events, are very like the ones you see at the Olympics. Other sports have been adapted to make them more suitable for disabled athletes. Five-a-side blind football is one of these. A few Paralympic sports, such as boccia (see page 15) are only played by athletes with disabilities.

THE PARALYMPICS TODAY
For the 2020 Tokyo Paralympics, 22 sports were included in the programme. Some of these sports include lots of different events. The two biggest sports are athletics with 168 events and swimming with 164. In the Winter Paralympics in 2022 there will be six or seven sports.

"In terms of missing half an arm, I don't see that as a disability because it hasn't stopped me doing anything in life so far."
– Matt Cowdrey, Australian swimmer.

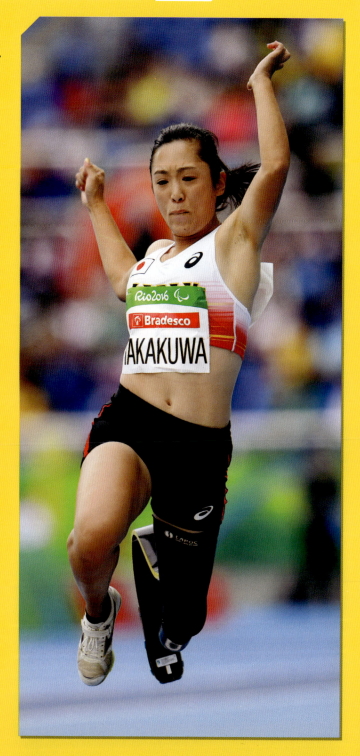

Right: Saki Takakuwa of Japan takes part in the final of the long jump competition at the 2016 Paralympics in Rio de Janeiro.

PARALYMPICS MILESTONES

1948 — STOKE MANDEVILLE, UK
The Wheelchair Games, a sports competition for British veterans with spinal injuries, is held.

1952 — STOKE MANDEVILLE, UK
The Wheelchair Games is held again, this time with Dutch and Israeli athletes also competing.

1960 — ROME
The first official Paralympic Games is held, open to athletes from any country but still wheelchair-only.

1976 — TORONTO/ORNSKOLDSVIK
Toronto holds the first Paralympics open to non-wheelchair athletes. The first Winter Paralympics take place in Ornskoldsvik, Sweden

AMAZING MOMENT
Károly TÁKACS

Athletes with disabilities sometimes compete at the Olympic Games. In fact, before the Paralympics began, they had no choice.

In 1948 and 1952, a Hungarian soldier called Károly Tákacs competed in the pistol shooting. Tákacs had been a top-level right-handed shooter, but his right hand was damaged by a faulty grenade. Tákacs taught himself to shoot left-handed, then won gold at two Olympics.

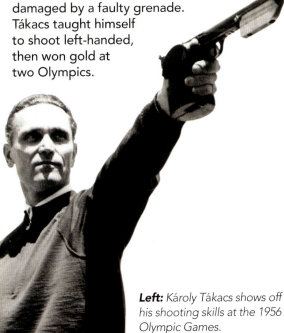

Left: Károly Tákacs shows off his shooting skills at the 1956 Olympic Games.

SUMMER SPORTS 2020

 ARCHERY
 ATHLETICS
 BADMINTON (new for 2020)
 BOCCIA
 CANOE

 CYCLING (track and road)
 EQUESTRIAN
 FOOTBALL 5-A-SIDE
 GOALBALL
 JUDO

 POWERLIFTING
 ROWING
 SHOOTING
 SITTING VOLLEYBALL
 SWIMMING

 TABLE TENNIS
 TAEKWONDO (new for 2020)
 TRIATHLON
 WHEELCHAIR BASKETBALL
 WHEELCHAIR FENCING

 WHEELCHAIR RUGBY

 WHEELCHAIR TENNIS

WINTER SPORTS 2022

 ALPINE SKIING

 BIATHLON
 CROSS-COUNTRY SKIING
 ICE HOCKEY
 SNOWBOARD
 CURLING

PARALYMPIC CLASSIFICATION

In many Paralympic sports, athletes with similar levels of ability are grouped together. This is called classification. The idea is to make the competition fairer.

IMPAIRMENTS

Ten types of disability or impairment are recognised by the International Paralympic Committee (IPC), the organisation in charge of the Games:

- eight different kinds of physical impairment
- visual impairment
- intellectual impairment.

Within categories of impairment there can be sub-groups. Athletes with cerebral palsy, for example, may be put into different sub-groups depending on how seriously the condition affects their ability to do sport.

Sports such as swimming and athletics are open to all categories. Other sports – equestrian and cycling, for example – only allow some categories to compete. A few, such as goalball, are for one category of athlete.

Below: *Wheelchair basketball players from Argentina (in blue) and Brazil (shooting) battle it out at the 2016 Paralympics.*

AMAZING MOMENT
Alex ZANARDI

Alex Zanardi was a successful racing driver in Formula 1 and the CART championship throughout the 1990s. After a terrible crash in 2001, both his legs had to be amputated.

Zanardi continued to drive racing cars, but also decided to become a handcycling racer. By 2011 he was good enough to win the New York Marathon. Next stop: the 2012 Paralympics. There, at the age of 45, Zanardi won gold in both the handcycling time trial and the road race.

Left: *Alex Zanardi of Italy races at the London 2012 Paralympics.*

DIFFERENCES BETWEEN SPORTS

Not all Paralympic sports put athletes into categories, but most do. The classifications are based on whether the athlete's impairment makes their sport harder to do. Rifle shooting, for example, is separated into:

- athletes with lower-limb disabilities, who are able to hold a rifle without help (class SH1)
- athletes with upper-limb disabilities, who need a shooting stand to hold up the rifle (class SH2).

The same disability affects different sports in different ways. Because of this, each sport has its own classification system.

❝ Usually people treat para athletes as an example of overcoming challenges. But no, we are athletes who do our best to be able to develop and succeed in our life projects, like anyone else. ❞
– Leomon Moreno, Brazilian goalball player

CLASSIFICATION

Classifiers are officials who look at what the athlete can and cannot do, and how it will affect their sporting performance. Then they decide which classification athletes should compete in.

In some sports, an athlete's classification is constantly being reviewed – even once they arrive at the competition. For the 2016 Paralympics, though, the IPC decided that there would be no reclassifications at the Games.

Right *Brazil 2016: goal! The ball hits the back of the net during a goalball match between Brazil and the USA.*

7

ARCHERY

The skills on show in para archery are amazing. It is not unusual to see someone shooting at a target 50 metres away ... while holding the bow with their foot.

Above: Matt Stutzman of the USA holds the bow with his right foot. Stutzman pulls the bowstring back with a device attached to his right shoulder and uses his jaw to release the arrow.

Left: Recurve bows get part of their power from the way the tips curve away from the archer.

CLASSIFICATION

There are three classifications for archery: ST (standing) athletes compete while standing; W1 (wheelchair 1) athletes are seated and have impairment that affects their arms, legs and trunk; W2 (wheelchair 2) athletes are seated and have an impairment that affects their legs and trunk.

TYPES OF BOW

Paralympic archers use two types of bow. Recurve bows need a lot of strength to pull back, but are powerful. Recurve archers shoot at a target 1.22 metres across from 70 metres away. Compound bows get part of their power from a system of pulleys. This makes it easier to pull back the bowstring, which is good for archers whose upper bodies are not as strong. Compound archers shoot at an 80 cm target from 50 metres away.

COMPETITION FORMAT AND SCORING

In archery, the targets contain 10 circles. Hitting the inner circle scores 10 points, and every circle further out wins one point less.

In individual recurve-bow matches, archers compete in pairs. Each shoots three arrows: the six together are known as a 'set'. The archer with the highest score wins the set and gets two points. If the scores are tied, they get a point each. The winner is the archer with most points after five sets.

Individual compound-bow matches have different scoring. They last 15 arrows per archer and the one with the highest total score wins.

8

SHOOTING

To be a good shot, you must use special techniques to slow your heartbeat and relax. Only then can your shooting be as accurate as possible.

CLASSIFICATION

There are two shooting classifications: SH1 athletes can support the weight of their gun without a shooting stand and use a rifle or pistol; SH2 athletes use a stand for support because of an impairment affecting one or both arms, and shoot using a rifle.

Left: In air rifle contests, the bullseye at the very centre measures just half a millimetre across – about the same as the full stop at the end of this sentence.

Below: New Zealand's Michael Johnson competes at the 2012 London Paralympics.

SCORING

The target is made up of ten circles, with a shot in the inner circle scoring 10. The 10 rings are each divided into 10: so, for example, a shot that is right in the middle of the centre circle will score 10.9. One right on the outside of that ring scores only 10.

QUALIFICATION AND FINALS

All the shooters take part in a qualification round. The top eight take part in the final. After they have all shot, the one with the lowest score is knocked out. They all shoot again and the same thing happens. This goes on until only two are left, fighting for gold or silver.

PARALYMPIC SUPERSTAR
Michael JOHNSON

CURRENT MEDAL COUNT

BORN
1973, Auckland, New Zealand

DISABILITY
Spinal cord injury

Despite only having taken up shooting in 2001, Johnson won gold at the 2004 Paralympics. Since then he has never been out of New Zealand's team.

What made you take up shooting?
[It] is one of the few sports which integrates ... able-bodied with disability and my goal was to try and beat the able-bodied guys.

Why do you love the sport so much?
[You] need to be quite patient and consistent. I also like the fact it has allowed me to travel the world and make so many friends, and I still feel I'm improving as a shooter.

ATHLETICS

The first time that people watch para athletics, they are often astounded. Until you see it, it can be hard to believe the speeds and heights that para athletes can reach!

EVENTS

Anyone who has watched athletics at the Olympics will recognise most of the events at the Paralympics. The biggest difference is the use of wheelchairs, prosthetic limbs (see p.12) or guides to make it possible for the athletes to compete.

CLASSIFICATION

Athletics classifications are separated into T (track) and F (field). Each athlete is given two numbers. The first shows what type of impairment they have. The second number shows how badly the athlete is affected, with lower numbers for the most difficult impairments.

WHEEL POWER

The first Paralympics was for wheelchair athletes only, and wheelchair sports and athletes are still a big part of the Paralympics. In track athletics, wheelchair design can be very important. Lighter, more aerodynamic wheelchairs can give an athlete a big advantage.

INCREASE IN PARALYMPIC ATHLETICS COMPETITION 1960–2008

Above: In 1960 31 para athletes participated in the Paralympic Games; by 2008 1,028 para athletes took part!

BORN
1976, Nottingham, UK

CURRENT MEDAL COUNT

0 2 1

DISABILITY
Born without lower legs

PARALYMPIC SUPERSTAR
Richard
WHITEHEAD

Richard Whitehead first appeared at the 2006 Winter Paralympics as a member of the ice-sledge hockey team, but later switched to athletics. Whitehead is a 'blade runner': he uses springy blades in place of his lower legs.

In 2010 Whitehead broke the world marathon record, but with no marathon event for his classification at the Paralympics, he switched to track sprinting. In 2012 and 2016 he won gold in the T42 200 metres.

What made you want to run marathons?
As a youngster, I was inspired by a Canadian athlete called Terry Fox … After losing his limb Terry attempted to run from the east to the west of Canada. His strength and determination was [my] inspiration.

What has been your career highlight so far?
Winning gold in front of a home crowd at London 2012. [I also] smashed the T42 200 metre world record with a time of 24.38 seconds. That was a pretty good day!

Do you have any quirky athletics habits?
I've got a lucky pair of underpants. I've run all my marathons in them … they're definitely worn in now!

Left: *Richard storms to victory in the men's 200 m T42 final at the 2016 Paralympics.*

PROSTHETICS

A prosthetic is an artificial body part. In track events, athletes with part of one or both legs missing wear blades – curved pieces of carbon-fibre, which attach to the runner's upper leg and replace the lower part. In field events, athletes are allowed to choose whether or not to wear a prosthetic leg.

Above: Para athletes can choose the form of prosthetic that they prefer – and which helps them to go faster!

GUIDES AND CALLERS

On the track, blind and visually impaired athletes sometimes have sighted guides helping them. They can use bits of rope or other devices to link them with their guide. They have to stay connected until no more than 10 metres from the line. After that, the blind athlete has to overtake and cross the line first, or they will be disqualified.

A noise-making device or a sighted 'caller' is sometimes used to help blind or partially sighted field athletes. The noise shows the take-off zone in jumping events or the target area for throws.

Right: Blind Brazilian para athlete Lorena Spoladore runs with the aid of a sighted guide.

TRIATHLON

Triathlon is a new Paralympic sport, as it first appeared at the Games in 2016. The event is a traditional swim/bike/run, but there are a few special things about a Paralympic triathlon.

CLASSIFICATION

Triathlon is open to wheelchair athletes (PT1), those with either minor or major limb impairments (PT2 and PT4), people with brain/nervous system disabilities (PT2) and those with visual impairment (PT5).

DISTANCES

All Paralympic triathlon racers do a 750 metre swim, a 20 km bike and a 5 km run. Athletes in PT1, PT2 and PT4 classes are allowed help from 'handlers', who do things like removing wetsuits and helping the athlete move from hand bike to wheelchair.

EQUIPMENT

Depending on their classification, para triathletes are allowed to use different kinds of equipment:

- PT1 athletes swim, use a hand bike for the ride, then use a racing wheelchair for the run section.

- PT2 competitors have either severe impairments (such as a double leg amputation below the knee) or a severe impairment of their brain or nervous system. PT4 triathletes have less severe impairments, such as a below-elbow arm amputation. Both categories use a normal bike for the cycle section, but adaptations (such as wearing a prosthetic leg) are allowed.

- PT5 racers have visual impairments. They are allowed to compete alongside a sighted guide, and in the bike section they ride a tandem.

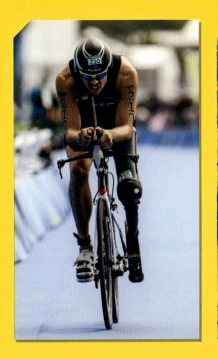

Far left: German para athlete Stefan Loesler takes part in the cycling leg of the PT2 men's triathlon at the Rio Paralympics.

Left: Visually impaired para athlete Alison Patrick competes in the 2016 PT5 triathlon with the help of a guide.

BADMINTON

Badminton was first added to the list of Paralympic sports for the Tokyo 2020 Games. Para badminton is especially popular in Asia, but it is played in at least 63 countries.

CLASSIFICATION

Para badminton has six classes in total: two for wheelchair badminton, two for people with leg impairments who stand to play, one for arm impairments and one for players who are particularly short.

TOP DRAW

Badminton is sure to be a big draw at the 2020 Paralympics. It is one of the most popular sports in Japan, where the Games are being held. The competition includes singles (with one player on each side), doubles (for two players on each side) and mixed doubles (with a male and female player on each side).

RULES

Most rules are almost the same as at the Olympics. Players play three games. A game is won by scoring 21 points. The first to win two games is the winner.

There are a few special rules, though. In wheelchair singles events, only half the width of the court is used. When they hit the shuttlecock, part of the player's trunk must be touching the seat of the wheelchair.

Para badminton is divided into three categories (standing upper, standing lower, and wheelchair) according to the extent of the athletes' impairment, and further into six classes according to the level of the athletes' impairment.

Above: *Thailand's Sujirat Pookkham stretches for the shuttlecock during a singles match at the Asian Para Games in 2018.*

BOCCIA

Boccia is one of the only Paralympic sports that is not also played at the Olympics. The other is goalball.

CLASSIFICATION

Boccia is played by wheelchair athletes. There are four different classifications, which depend on what the player physically can and cannot do. All events are mixed, with men and women competing together.

RULES

Boccia is similar to the French sport pétanque or the winter sport curling, but it is played with soft balls on a flat surface.

The game starts with a white target ball called a 'jack' being thrown. Each player then aims to throw, roll or kick their own balls as close to this as possible. Athletes in some classifications release the ball down a ramp. The player with the ball closest to the jack wins that 'end'. They get one point for the winning ball. They get another point for every other ball closer to the jack than their opponent's closest one.

Matches can be between two players or between teams of players. Individual and pairs matches are played over four 'ends', team matches last six.

Left: *Each player is given a space at the end of the court, which they must stay inside during the match.*

AMAZING MOMENT

Worawut **SAENGAMPA** & Watcharaphon **VONGSA**

Thailand is one of the strongest countries in Paralympic boccia. In fact, it won medals in four of the seven categories in 2016.

In the 2016 Paralympic final, two Thai players were up against each other. Watcharaphon Vongsa was world number 1 and had won his semi-final 11–0. Worawut Saengampa was younger and had won his semi-final 10–1. It was an extremely tight match, but in the end Vongsa triumphed 5–4.

Left: *Overcome with emotion, Watcharaphon Vongsa celebrates winning gold in the boccia final at the 2016 Paralympics.*

CANOEING

Canoe racing first appeared at the Paralympics in 2016. People watching it for the first time found out that it was just as exciting as the same event at the Olympics.

CLASSIFICATION

Canoe athletes are given classification points according to how well they are able to move their legs and torso. The classifiers also watch them paddling as part of the assessment. Higher points show that an athlete has a less severe impairment.

There are 3 classes in Paralympic canoe racing: KL1 for athletes with up to 3 points, KL2 for 4–7 points and KL3 for 8 or 9 points.

PADDLING STYLE

Although it is called 'canoe racing', the athletes actually kayak: they use a long paddle with a blade at each end. Canoeing uses a shorter paddle with a blade at only one end. In other competitions, para canoeists sometimes use a boat called a va'as, which has a small outrigger and is propelled with a single-bladed paddle. These were not used in 2016, but may appear at future Paralympics.

AMAZING MOMENT
Curtis MCGRATH

McGrath is a former soldier in the Australian Army. Both his legs had to be partly amputated in 2012, after an explosion in Afghanistan. He later said, "Even when I was on the stretcher getting carried to the medevac chopper I said I was going to be in the Paralympics."

In 2016 his prediction came true. Not only was he at the Paralympics, he won the KL2 200 metres – in a world record time.

Above: Anne Dickins powers towards gold at the 2016 Paralympics. Her medal was Team GB's 100th of the Games.

Right: Curtis McGrath: as well as being a Paralympic canoe champion, he is a top-level para swimmer.

COURSE AND COMPETITION FORMAT

The racers paddle on flat water along a straight course. They start together and each paddles down his or her own lane. The lanes are marked out by small coloured buoys. The first racer to cross the finish line wins.

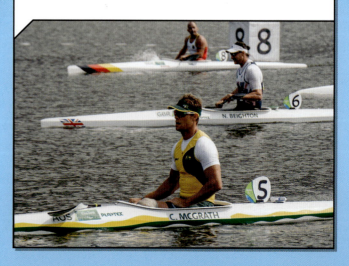

ROWING

Rowing is one of the most exhausting sports. To cover the 2,000 metre course in the fastest time, the athletes need strength, power and endurance.

CATEGORIES

There are three different types of race at the Paralympics, each one for athletes with different types of impairment. See the Events section for more information.

EVENTS

The rowers compete in either sweep, with one oar per rower, or scull, with two oars. There are four rowing events at the Paralympics.

- Mixed coxed four, which is a sweep event. The rowers have movement in the legs, torso and/or arms, and up to two people in each boat can have a visual impairment. Each boat has a four-person crew of two men and two women. There is also a guide called a cox lying in the front of the boat giving directions. (The cox does not have to have an impairment and can be male or female.)

- Double scull, with two rowers per boat, one male and one female. The double scull is for rowers who have movement in their torso and arms, but not their legs.

- Men's and women's single scull, for a single rower using two oars. This event is for rowers who have full movement only in their arms and shoulders. The athletes are strapped to seats that are fixed in place, and the boats are fitted with small outriggers so that they cannot capsize.

Below: *Josiane Lima of Brazil shows off her rowing muscles, after winning gold alongside Michel Pessanha in the mixed double sculls.*

CYCLING

There are two kinds of cycling at the Paralympics: road and track. It is one of the most popular sports; only athletics and swimming have more events.

CLASSIFICATION

Athletes compete on different bikes depending on their impairment (see Equipment for more information). For each event there are 'classes' for different levels of impairment. There are five classes in handcycling, two in tricycle and five in bicycle. There are also three classes for tandem, but all compete in one event.

EQUIPMENT

In road cycling there are four types of bike. The first are bicycles, sometimes modified for riders with prosthetic limbs. Tandems are for riders with visual impairments: they sit behind a sighted pilot and are sometimes called 'stokers'. Hand bikes are used by amputees and paraplegic athletes. Tricycles are for athletes with impaired balance and/or coordination. In track cycling, only bicycles or tandems are used.

ROAD RACING

The three Paralympic road-racing events are:
- Road race, over distances of 30–120 km. All the riders start together and the first to cross the finish line wins
- Individual time trial (over 20–35 km). Cyclists leave one at a time and race against the clock, with the fastest time winning
- Team relay, which is for handcyclists only. The teams have three athletes from different classes, and can be men and women.

TRACK CYCLING

Like road racing, track cycling has three events:
- Time trial, a race against the clock over 500 metres or 1 km
- Individual pursuit over 3 or 4 km. The athletes start on opposite sides of the track: to win they must either catch their opponent or do the fastest time
- Team sprint, with three riders racing for three laps – each has to lead for one lap before leaving the race.

Left: Tandem bikes are used by visually impaired Paralympic cyclists. The para athlete has a sighted rider aboard to steer the bike.

BORN
1976, Greenville, USA

CURRENT MEDAL COUNT

0 2 0

DISABILITY
Nerve damage and visual impairment

PARALYMPIC SUPERSTAR
Shawn MORELLI

Morelli is a former engineer officer in the US Army. She was injured by a bomb in 2007 while in Afghanistan. She lost the sight in her left eye and suffered neck and nerve damage. In 2016 Morelli won gold in the road time trial and the track pursuit at the Rio Paralympics. She also came tenth in the road race.

When did you start bike racing?
My first local race was in 2010. I progressed pretty quickly and ended up racing Nationals in 2012 … I've been training and racing seriously ever since.

What's the training like for para-cycling?
I train every day. Sometimes I have up to three sessions a day between cycling, and strength and conditioning. I take rest days when I need them.
  There is always a level of pain you have to work through when you're competing at a high level with existing injuries. Those injuries make every day training and racing a little bit harder than for able-bodied athletes.

What achievement are you most proud of?
Teaching my dog to catch a Frisbee!

Left: *Shawn Morelli of the USA celebrates winning gold in the 3,000 m individual pursuit at the 2016 Paralympics.*

FOOTBALL 5-A-SIDE

Try wrapping a scarf around your eyes so that you cannot see, then playing football.* It will give you some idea of how tricky this sport (also called 'blind football') can be.

CATEGORIES

There are two categories for players. All outfield players have to be classed as blind; they wear blackout masks to make sure none of them can see anything. The goalkeeper may be fully or partially sighted.

RULES AND SAFETY

Of course, the rules are not exactly the same as regular 5-a-side football. Players use a special ball with a noise-making device inside it, so they can hear where it is. Behind their goal, each team has a guide. He or she constantly gives information about where the players are on the pitch and how close they are to others. The team coach and goalkeeper are also allowed to give instructions.

When they are getting close to someone else or the ball, the players have to keep saying 'voy' (or a similar word) to warn opponents they are coming.

NON-STOP (QUIET) ACTION

A Paralympic 5-a-side pitch is 40 metres long and 20 metres wide, and is surrounded by a wall. The wall is there to keep the ball and players safely on the pitch. Unlike in regular football, there are no throw-ins because the ball has gone out. There is also no offside rule. The action is fast-moving and almost non-stop.

One big difference from regular football is that Paralympic 5-a-side is played in near silence. The crowd has to keep quiet so that the players can hear the ball, each other and the instructions being shouted at them. When a goal is scored and the crowd erupts, it can come as quite a shock!

Left: *Team GB shoots and Turkey defends in their match at the 2012 Paralympics.*

*Actually, don't: you'll hurt yourself. Do this as a thought experiment instead.

PARALYMPIC SUPERSTAR
RICARDINHO

BORN
1988, Osório, Brazil

CURRENT MEDAL COUNT

0 4 0

DISABILITY
Visual impairment

Brazilian Ricardo Alves – known to everyone as Ricardinho – is probably the greatest football 5-a-side player ever.

By 2016, Ricardinho had taken part in:

- The 2004 Athens Paralympics: the final against Argentina was a draw, and Brazil won 3–2 on penalties
- The 2008 Beijing Games, where they won 2–1 against the hosts, China
- The London 2012 Paralympics, where Brazil beat France 2–0.

To cap all his achievements so far, Ricardinho captained the Brazil team at the 2016 Paralympics in Rio de Janeiro, Brazil – and scored the winning goal in the final.

Below: Ricardinho holds off two – no, three! – defenders during the 2016 Paralympics in his home country, Brazil.

GOALBALL

Goalball was developed as a form of rehabilitation for visually impaired soldiers after the Second World War (1939–1945). It first appeared at the Paralympics in 1976.

Below: *Goalball players wear black-out masks while on court. There is a strict rule that these may not be touched except with the referee's permission.*

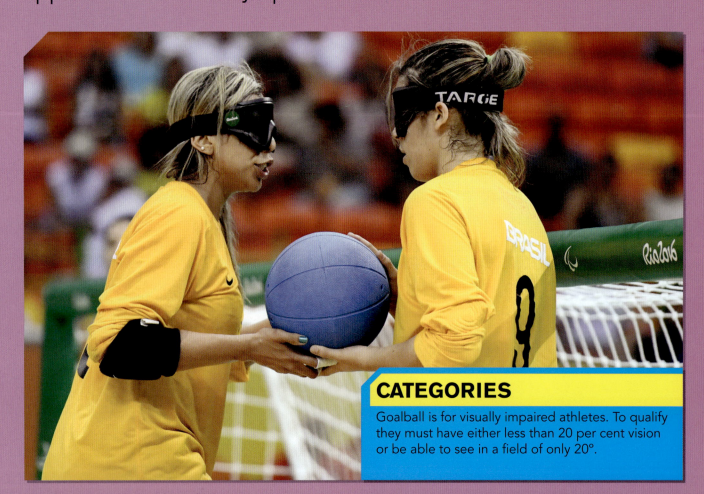

CATEGORIES
Goalball is for visually impaired athletes. To qualify they must have either less than 20 per cent vision or be able to see in a field of only 20°.

AIM OF THE GAME
The aim of goalball – not surprisingly – is to score goals. This is done by throwing the ball underarm at the opposition goal. There are three players per team on court. If a defender stops the ball, he or she has up to 10 seconds to launch an attack.

The top players make one of the key attacking skills look simple, but it is actually very difficult. They disguise their attack by spinning through 360° before releasing the ball towards the opposition goal. This makes it much harder to hear where the ball is coming from.

COURT AND EQUIPMENT
Play takes place on a court measuring 18 x 9 metres, with goals all the way across the court at each end. There are strings on the court lines. which the players can reach down to feel as a way of checking where they are. The ball is hard and rubbery, with two bells inside to help the players hear where it is. As in football 5-a-side, the crowd has to stay completely silent while the game is on.

BORN
1993, Brasília, Brazil

CURRENT MEDAL COUNT

1 0 1

DISABILITY
Visual impairment

PARALYMPIC SUPERSTAR
Leomon MORENO

Until recently, Brazil was not one of the world's top goalball teams. It is now, though – and Leomon Moreno is part of the reason why.

In the 2012 Paralympics, Moreno's goalscoring helped Brazil win silver: their first ever Paralympic medal. Four years later, at the 2016 Paralympics, Moreno scored 27 goals – among them the winning goal in Brazil's 6–5 victory in the bronze-medal match against Sweden.

Below: Brazilian players celebrate their 2016 bronze medal. Moreno is second from the left.

How did it feel to be top scorer again at the 2018 World Championships?
I was watching the games and saw that many [other players] were scoring numerous goals and I was not even paying attention to mine… [But] being the top scorer in the competition was very important, because I had already been the top scorer of the last World Championships back in 2014. To keep this record is a difficult thing to do.

Are the preparations for 2020 going well?
I'm dedicated to training with the team and we are achieving results … We want nothing but the gold medal at the next Paralympics Games. We already have one silver and one bronze, and now we want gold.

AMAZING MOMENT
Sevda ALTUNOLUK

Sevda Altunoluk of Turkey is one of the best goal-scorers in goalball. At the 2016 Paralympics, Altunoluk scored 33 goals to get her team to the gold-medal match against China. She scored another three goals in the final, and Turkey won its first Paralympic goalball medal, with a 4–1 victory.

Right: Sevda Altunoluk serves against China in the 2016 gold-medal match.

JUDO

Until 2020, judo was the only combat sport in the Paralympics. Because judo players constantly hold on to one another, it is a good combat sport for visually impaired athletes.

CATEGORIES

Judo is for visually impaired athletes only. They are given impairment categories ranging from B1 for total blindness to B3 for weak vision, but these do not affect who they fight or the medal categories. Instead the players fight in weight divisions, just as in regular judo.

The only difference from regular judo is that before starting to grapple, players must hold on to their opponent's lapel with one hand and their sleeve with the other. When they are still, the referee says, 'Hajime!' – and the fight is on.

AMAZING MOMENT
Beijing 2008

China had high hopes for judo success at its home Paralympics. Even the biggest judo fan could not have imagined what the women's team would achieve, though. The team won gold in four of the six weight divisions: -48 kg, -52 kg, -57 kg and over 70 kg.

Below: Wang Lijing of China, 2008 Paralympic gold medallist in the women's -57 kg category.

Above: Spectacular Paralympic judo action.

JUDO RULES

The rules of Paralympic judo are almost the same as regular judo. Matches last four minutes. Players win by throwing their opponent or pinning them to the ground. Throwing them cleanly so that they land flat on their back scores ippon, one whole point, and wins the match. A throw that puts your opponent partly on their back scores waza-ari, half a point. Two waza-ari win the match.

24

TAEKWONDO

Taekwondo only began to develop as a sport for para athletes in 2005. By 2020, though, it was ready to become part of the programme for the Tokyo Games.

CATEGORIES

Paralympic taekwondo is for athletes with upper-limb impairments. The fighters use their arms and hands for defence, so they are divided into four classes, from K41 to K44. K41 is for athletes with the greatest degree of arm or hand impairment. Men and women each compete in one of three weight divisions.

KICKING AND SCORING

Because the key technique in taekwondo is kicking, the sport is suitable for athletes with arm impairments. One difference from regular taekwondo is that kicks to the head are not allowed. The fighters must aim their kicks at the other fighter's torso. The number of points they win for a successful kick depends on the difficulty of the technique they use:

- Two points are awarded for a valid kick
- Three points for a kick involving a 180° turn
- Four points for a spinning kick that pivots from a rear kick, adding up to a total 360° turn.

The four-point kick only exists in para taekwondo. It is an exciting technique, with such a big score that it can change the course of a fight.

TWO FORMS

There are two different forms of para taekwondo. Gyeorugi is for athletes with arm impairments. Poomsae is for athletes with intellectual impairments. At the moment, only Gyeorugi appears at the Paralympics.

Right: Fighters from Mongolia (blue) and Uzbekistan at the seventh World Para Taekwondo Championships in 2017. Until their sport became part of the Paralympics in 2020, the World Championships was the biggest competition for taekwondo para athletes.

POWERLIFTING

Powerlifting is a test of upper body strength. Some Paralympic competitors are so strong that they can lift over three times their own weight!

CLASSIFICATION

This event is open to athletes with a range of different physical disabilities and impairments, but athletes compete with others in the same weight category as them. There are 10 different weight categories for men and 10 for women.

TECHNIQUE

Powerlifters lie on their back with their arms straight up, holding a metal bar with weights attached to each end. They hold the bar still until the referee signals, then lower it to their chest, hold it still and lift it back up. When the bar is still, the referee says 'Rack' and the bar can be put safely back into its holding rack.

COMPETITION AND SCORING

After each lift, three judges decide whether it was done properly. If they think it was OK, they signal with a white light. If not, the signal is red. A powerlifter needs two white lights for his or her lift to count. Two or more red lights mean the lift will not count.

Athletes are usually allowed three attempts, at any weight they choose. After each round, the weight is increased. This continues until the bar is so heavy that only one person can lift it. He or she is the winner. The judges sometimes allow a fourth attempt, if the athlete is trying for a world record. This fourth lift does not count as part of the competition.

Below: *Japan's Tetsuo Nishizaki competes in the men's -54 kg weight division at the 2016 Paralympics.*

BORN
1998, Osnavieh, Iran

CURRENT MEDAL COUNT

0 2 0

DISABILITY
Born with leg impairment

PARALYMPIC SUPERSTAR
Siamand RAHMAN

Siamand Rahman is a ground-breaking athlete, the first para powerlifter to break the able-bodied powerlifting world record.

Rahman first won gold at the 2012 Paralympics. In 2016 he was hoping to win again. As an increasingly amazed crowd looked on, he started by easily lifting 270 kg. Next he broke his own world record by lifting 300 kg. The crowd roared: at the time this was 10 kg more than the record for an able-bodied lifter. Rahman wasn't done: he went on to make two more lifts, of 305 kg and 310 kg.

How did you get into powerlifting?
The people around encouraged me, especially my father and mother. The kindness and respect from the people of my country made me continue, despite the barriers in my way.

What did it feel like to win by lifting over 300 kg?
I had a good feeling! I was very delighted and happy that I could have the Iranian flag hoisted at such an important competition and to make the people of my country happy.

What are your aims for the Paralympics?
To have a memorable experience … and, of course, bring home the gold medal. I will definitely be trying to break the world record at the Tokyo 2020 Games.

Left: Day seven of the 2016 Paralympics in Rio, and Siamand Rahman celebrates gold in the 107+ kg weight division. He not only won the contest, but also set a new world record.

SITTING VOLLEYBALL

Sitting volleyball is one of the most popular Paralympic sports, with over 10,000 players in more than 75 countries. Top players need speed, strength, endurance and quick thinking.

CLASSIFICATION

For each team, four players on court must have an qualifying impairment. These include being an amputee or lacking muscular strength or movement in a joint. The impaired players are classified minimally disabled (MD) or disabled (D). Teams can include two MDs, but only one is allowed on court at a time.

AIM OF THE GAME

The aim is to keep the ball off the ground in your court and force the opposition to let it fall to the ground in theirs. Teams can hit the ball no more than three times before it passes back across the net. Each time a team lets the ball touch the ground or puts it out of play, the opposition gets a point.

RULES

Teams can include up to 12 players, with six on court at any one time. When playing the ball, players' bottoms must be in contact with the floor.

Two metres from the net are 'attack lines', which create attack zones. Three players in each team play in their attack zone. Only these players can block attacks. Unlike in standing volleyball, defenders are allowed to attack or block a serve.

SCORING

Matches are the best of five sets. In the first four sets, you must get 25 points (and be two points ahead of the other team) to win. In the fifth set, the first team to score 15 points wins.

Below: Great Britain players block the ball during their match against Ukraine at the 2012 Paralympics. Meanwhile, officials watch carefully for rule infringements.

WHEELCHAIR BASKETBALL

Wheelchair basketball is fast and furious. There are lots of points scored and plenty of high-speed end-to-end action.

CLASSIFICATION

Wheelchair basketball players are separated into eight 'sport classes', ranging from 1.0 to 4.5. Class 1 has the most impairment, class 4.5 the least. The sport classes of the five players on court must add up to no more than 14.

AIM AND RULES

The aim is to score points by passing the ball into the opposition's basket. The team to score most points wins.

The rules are very similar to standing basketball. The biggest difference is in dribbling, when players can have the ball on their lap or in their hand for two pushes of the wheelchair. Then they must bounce the ball on the ground, or they have committed a 'travelling' foul.

PARALYMPIC SUPERSTAR
Rose HOLLERMANN

CURRENT MEDAL COUNT
0 1 0

Hollermann first played wheelchair basketball at the Paralympics when she was just 16, in 2012. The USA team finished fourth. In 2016 Hollerman was again selected: this time the team won gold.

BORN
1995, Mankato, USA

DISABILITY
Part paralysed from the waist down

You play lots of other sports: which do you like best?
I really love swimming … Tennis, track, field, archery … sled hockey, cross-country skiing … basically anything, and everything.

You're a student at University of Texas-Arlington. Did you have to ditch school for the Paralympics?
Yes – we missed a lot of classes! There was definitely a lot of material to catch up with, but we are grateful that our teachers are very supportive.

It was worth it?
It meant everything to me.

Right: Rose Hollermann holds the US flag in the air, after her team's win against Germany in the 2016 Paralympic gold-medal match.

SWIMMING

Swimming has been part of the Paralympics since the first Games in 1960. It has appeared at every Paralympics since then.

CLASSIFICATIONS

Swimming events have letters S (for freestyle, butterfly and backstroke), SN (breaststroke) and SM (medley).

They also have numbers: from 1–10 for physical impairments, 11–13 for visual impairments and 14 for intellectual impairment. Lower numbers are for greater impairments.

Above: *Swimming is one of the biggest sports at the Paralympics. At every Games it gets more popular.*

EVENTS

The main events are similar to regular swimming. The strokes are freestyle, backstroke, butterfly, breaststroke and individual medley. The shortest races are 50 metres, the longest is the 400 metres freestyle. There are also freestyle and medley relays.

One race that is unique to para swimming is the 150 metres medley. Most medley races are swum butterfly/backstroke/breaststroke/front crawl. In the 150m medley, though, swimmers do backstroke, breaststroke and freestyle. The event is for athletes with severe impairments, and the way they are able to adapt their swimming to their impairments is inspiring to watch.

"I don't know whether to laugh, jump or throw up. It's my first event and I've broken the world record and won. I'm in heaven."
– Canada's Aurélie Rivard after winning the 50 metres freestyle in 2016.

Below: *Swimmers surge through the water in a heat for the men's 50 m freestyle.*

BORN
1993, Christchurch, New Zealand

CURRENT MEDAL COUNT

0 9 6

DISABILITY
Below-the-knee amputee

PARALYMPIC SUPERSTAR
Sophie PASCOE

Sophie became a national hero in New Zealand at the age of just 15. At the 2008 Paralympics she won three gold medals and one silver. Sophie went on to win six more gold medals at the 2012 and 2016 Games.

Sophie, what is a typical day for you?
It starts at 5.30 a.m. when the alarm goes off. I have a smoothie and some toast before heading for the pool for a two-hour swim session. After that I have a bigger breakfast, then go to physio, then a one-and-a-half-hour nap. I have lunch, go to the gym, have another snack, then I'm back in the pool for another two-hour swim session.

What do you find hardest about competing?
The toughest part is the holding room … it's where all the tactics happen and psyching out the other athletes. You need to be tactical and give off the right vibes. The swimming is easy: you trust your instincts that you've done enough.

What do you do when you're not swimming?
I love to spend time with family and friends, go shopping, going out for a coffee and going to the movies.

Left: Sophie proudly displays her silver medal for coming second in the women's 100 m freestyle at the 2016 Paralympics.

31

STARTS

In Paralympic swimming, three different starting positions are allowed. Swimmers can dive off the blocks from a standing position, like in non-Paralympic swimming races. They can also dive from a sitting position or start in the water.

In backstroke races, everyone starts in the water. Usually the swimmers start by holding a bar or grip on the starting platform. If their impairment means they cannot do this, they are allowed to use a belt, or grip a string or towel in their mouth.

TURNS, FINISHES AND TAPPERS

At turns and the finish in breaststroke and butterfly races, swimmers who cannot touch the end of the pool with their hand/s are allowed to finish using another part of their upper body. Some visually impaired swimmers cannot see the end of the pool, so they need a warning that they're getting close. This comes from a 'tapper' – a person standing at the end, who uses a long pole to tap the swimmer as they get near. Visually impaired athletes also have to find a way of swimming straight. They either use good technique or swim close enough to the lane line to feel where they are.

Above: The start of the gold-medal race in the men's 50 m freestyle at the Rio Paralympics.

Below: McClain Hermes of the USA is tapped on the head, warning her she is close to the end of the pool.

BORN
1994, Walsall, UK

CURRENT MEDAL COUNT

1 | 5 | 0

DISABILITY
Short stature

PARALYMPIC SUPERSTAR
Ellie SIMMONDS

Ellie Simmonds shot to fame at the Beijing 2008 Paralympics where, aged just 13, she won two gold medals. Simmonds took two more golds at the London 2012 Games. At the 2016 Games in Brazil she won another gold and a bronze medal.

How did things change for you after the 2008 Paralympics?
I was only 13, but I came away with two gold medals. I was so shocked and surprised to win. Later I won the Young Sports Personality of the Year and became the youngest person ever to get an MBE.

Do you get recognised in the street these days?
Yes. I never get asked for autographs, though, these days it's always selfies. I like that. I'm very sociable so I'm always happy to meet people.

Do you ever swim outside, away from the training pool?
I love the ocean and I'm passionate about conservation and the environment. I've swum with dolphins in Mozambique and with bull sharks off Mexico. They didn't tell me how dangerous the sharks were until after I got out.

Which other swimmers do you most admire?
When I met Michael Phelps, my absolute idol, I was totally starstruck. I did manage to get a few words out: we talked about what we were going to be doing for Christmas.

Left: Ellie Simmonds, back in London after the 2016 Paralympics, displays her medals to fans.

TABLE TENNIS

Table tennis is the third biggest Paralympic sport and one of the most competitive.

CLASSIFICATION

There are 11 different classes. Players with physical impairments are divided into standing and seated categories. Classes 1–5 are for seated athletes, 6–10 are for standing players. In each category, lower numbers are for those with the greatest impairments. Class 11 is for those with intellectual impairments.

RULES AND ADAPTATIONS

The basic rules are almost the same as in regular table tennis. Matches are the best of five sets. In each set the first player to score 11 points wins, as long as they are two points ahead.

There are some adaptations in para table tennis. Athletes who cannot start their serve with the ball in their hand are allowed to start with the ball in the crook of their elbow, or balanced on the racquet. Standing players can use supports such as crutches.

AMAZING MOMENT
Natalia PARTYKA

It is difficult to pick just one amazing moment out of Natalya Partyka's Paralympic career, because it has been full of them. The first was in 2000, when aged just 11, Natalia Partyka of Poland competed at her first Paralympics.

Partyka has been at every Games since, and has won four singles titles, plus a team gold at Rio 2016. She also competed at the Olympic Games in 2008, 2012 and 2016.

Below: Few athletes have competed at both the Paralympics and the Olympics. Poland's Natalia Partyka is one of them.

WHEELCHAIR TENNIS

Wheelchair tennis is a fast-moving version of the game. It is very similar to Olympic tennis, with a few rule changes to make it more suitable for athletes who use a wheelchair.

CLASSIFICATION

Athletes with impairments that affect two limbs compete in the open classes. There are open classes for men and women. If three or more limbs are affected, players compete in the quad class: men and women both compete in a single quad class.

EVENTS AND EQUIPMENT

There are six events in total: men's and women's singles, men's and women's doubles, quad singles and quad doubles. Players use special wheelchairs with the wheels angled inward at the top. The chairs are designed to stay upright during high-speed manoeuvres.

"Playing wheelchair tennis has given me so many great opportunities, and I'm hoping I can inspire others to get involved and enjoy sport as much I do."
– Alfie Hewett, Team GB wheelchair tennis star and Olympic medallist.

THE TWO-BOUNCE RULE

The biggest difference from Olympic tennis is that players can let the ball bounce twice before hitting it back across the net. The first bounce has to be inside the court, but the second can be outside.

SCORING

Matches are the best of three sets. Scoring is the same as in Olympic tennis. To win a set a player has to win six games and be at least two games in front. (If a set finishes 6–6, the players play a tie-break to decide the winner.) To win a game, a player must win four points and be at least two points ahead of their opponent.

Left: *Alfie Hewett of Great Britain celebrates winning a point in the Paralympics singles final.*

WHEELCHAIR FENCING

This is a lightning-fast battle of technique and tactics. The fencers' wheelchairs are fixed to the floor. This is so they can move their upper bodies quickly without their chair toppling over.

CLASSIFICATION

Wheelchair fencers are divided into two categories, A and B. A is for fencers with good control of their upper body and no impairment of their fencing arm. B is for fencers with more severe impairments.

CHAIR SETTING

The wheelchairs are set at an angle of 110° from the centre line of the fencing piste. The fencer with the shortest reach decides on the distance between chairs. It can be set at the length of the other fencer's reach or their own.

CHOOSE YOUR WEAPON

There are three different types of event, which depend on the weapon used:
- Epée is the heaviest weapon. In Epée, the whole body above the waist is a target.
- Foil is a light weapon derived from the court sword. The target area is the opponent's trunk.
- Sabre is a weapon based on a cavalry sword and fencers usually score hits with the edge of the weapon. The target area is anywhere above the waist.

AMAZING MOMENT
Beatrice VIO

At the age of 11, this Italian fencer had to have her legs amputated at the knee and arms at the forearm. She started to compete as a wheelchair fencer and by the age of 16 had won a World Cup event. At Rio 2016 Beatrice won gold in the individual foil.

Above: Fencing at the 2016 Paralympics.

Right: Italian Beatrice (Bebe) Vio has been fencing since she was just five years old.

WHEELCHAIR RUGBY

Wheelchair rugby was originally known as 'murderball'. This is a tough, fast sport in which tackling using your chair is allowed. (The chairs have to be especially strong to survive.)

CLASSIFICATION

This sport is for athletes with upper and lower limb impairments. Players are given a number from 0.5 to 3.5, with lower scores for the greatest impairment.

A SURPRISING SPORT

Wheelchair rugby is really more like a mash-up of rugby sevens, basketball and handball. Crashing your wheelchair into another is allowed (though dangerous contact is not) and so are forward passes. The rules encourage fast play and excitement.

TEAM NUMBERS

Teams are made up of 12 players, with only four on court at once. This is a mixed sport, so teams can include men and women. If the team is all-male, their impairments cannot add up to a number higher than 8. For every female team member, this number increases by 0.5.

RULES OF THE GAME

Wheelchair rugby is played on a court similar to a basketball court. Points are scored by carrying the ball across the opposition's goal line, with at least two wheels of your wheelchair on the ground.

Games last four eight-minute quarters. When they get the ball, a team's players have 12 seconds to get it out of their own half and 40 seconds to score. Otherwise, they hand over possession to the other team. Players must bounce or pass the ball within 10 seconds of getting it.

Left: *The wheelchairs used in wheelchair rugby have to be tough enough to survive a lot of knocks!*

SNOWBOARD

There are two types of snowboarding at the Winter Paralympics: snowboard cross and banked slalom. Whichever you watch, there are likely to be thrills, spills and slides galore.

Below: *Snowboard cross at the PyeongChang 2018 Paralympic Games: Carl Murphy of New Zealand leaps ahead of Alex Massie of Canada.*

CLASSIFICATION
There are three classes in para-snowboarding, two for leg impairments and one for arm impairments. Leg-impaired athletes are divided into severe and less-severe impairments.

SNOWBOARD CROSS
The most spectacular snowboard cross event is the head-to-head. The course for this goes down a series of drops, banked turns, slalom gates and gap jumps.

The riders start by making three runs down the course on their own. Their fastest time is counted, and the top 16 men and 8 women go through to the knockout stage. Here they race against each other, with the winner (and sometimes second place) getting through to the next round. This carries on until the medals are decided.

BANKED SLALOM
Riders get three attempts to get down a slalom course as fast as possible, weaving their way through a series of poles. The course usually goes down a sloping valley. There are plenty of bumps and dips to make things even more tricky. Each rider's fastest time counts and the medals are decided based on who is quickest.

BORN
1996, Baton Rouge, USA

CURRENT MEDAL COUNT

0 2 0

DISABILITY
Amputation of right leg above the knee

PARALYMPIC SUPERSTAR
Brenna HUCKABY

Huckaby is one of the biggest stars in para snowboarding. She took up snowboarding aged 15, and within four years was a double world champion. At the 2018 Paralympics she won gold in the snowboard cross and slalom.

How did you get into para snowboarding?
My whole life up until I was 14 I was a gymnast, but unfortunately that ended when I got osteosarcoma cancer, which resulted in a leg amputation. My hospital sent me on a rehabilitation ski trip, where I learned how to snowboard for the first time. The second I got on a snowboard I was like, 'Yep, this is my new thing.'

How do you feel about snowboarding now, looking back?
Snowboarding gave me the ability to not be great at something in the beginning, but work towards an overall goal of being great.

Did anyone ever try to tell you that you wouldn't succeed?
Not in snowboarding. I mean, I am always told AK [above-the-knee amputee] snowboarders will never be as good … but I constantly prove that wrong. I just work extra hard on the skills and movements people tell me are impossible.

What has your para sports experience so far taught you?
That you don't realise how strong you are, until being strong is the only option you have.

Left: Brenna Huckaby celebrates her win in snowboard cross at the 2018 Winter Paralympics.

ENDURANCE SKIING

Cross-country skiing is sometimes described as the toughest endurance sport there is. Cross-country and biathlon (which includes shooting) are among the hardest events at the Winter Paralympics.

CLASSIFICATION
Skiers in cross-country and biathlon are put into three main groups: standing, sitting and visually impaired. Within each group are categories for different types and levels of impairment. Visually impaired skiers race with a guide.

CROSS-COUNTRY SKIING
In cross-country skiing, the racers cannot rely on gravity to slide them down a hill. They have to power themselves around a course that has climbs, flat bits and downhills. There are three events each for men and women:

- A sprint of 1.1 km for sitting skiers and 1.5 km for standing
- A longer race of 7.5 km for women and 10 km for men (or for sitting skiers, 5 km and 7.5 km)
- The longest race, of 15 km for women and 20 km for men (for sitting skiers, 12 km and 15 km).

BIATHLON
Biathlon is a cross-country ski race in which the skiers stop and shoot at a target, then continue around the course. Shooting when you are trembling with effort is not easy! Visually impaired biathletes find the target by listening to a sound signal.

Top right: *The distances for sitting skiers are shorter because powering yourself around the course using only your arms and torso is extremely tiring.*

Right: *Clara Klug of Germany shoots during the visually impaired biathlon.*

BORN
1979, Calgary, Canada

CURRENT MEDAL COUNT

2 13 2

DISABILITY
Visual impairment

PARALYMPIC SUPERSTAR
Brian McKEEVER

Brian McKeever is the most successful Paralympic cross-country skier ever. At the 2018 Games he 'three-peated': he won all three men's individual gold medals for the third time.

How do you go about finding a guide to ski with?
It's actually really difficult to find somebody that's fast enough.

So you decided to use two guides?
Yes. In the past, if whoever was guiding me got a little tired, I could ski a little bit on my own and the guide could shortcut. With two guides I would never be on my own, there's always someone ready to step in and switch back and forth.

Do you keep count of your medals?
I don't. I'm always kind of surprised at the number. I always focus on the process: it's more on the training and how I can tweak that, how I can get a few more per cent out of my performance.

Describe the feeling of being at the Games.
It's a fantastic feeling. It's the pinnacle of para sport and it's what we aspire to achieve. It's very liberating as an athlete with a disability to see that there are no limits to the level of performance.

Left: Brian McKeever (left) and his guide, Graham Nishikawa, at the 2018 Winter Paralympics

ICE SPORTS

Two ice sports – wheelchair curling and ice hockey – have been part of the Paralympics for some time. In 2022 they may be joined by the high-speed, gravity-powered sport of bobsleigh.

CLASSIFICATION

In wheelchair curling and ice hockey, competitors must have an impairment affecting their legs. In ice hockey the impairment must be one that stops them playing regular ice hockey.

WHEELCHAIR CURLING

This is similar to the Olympic version. Each team slides stones down the ice into a target area called the 'house'. The aim is to get their stones closer to the middle of the target than the other team. As well as aiming for the centre of the house, players position stones to block their opponents.

AMAZING MOMENT
Sonja GAUDET

Gaudet (left; centre) has played in three Paralympics. She won gold in her very first Games, in 2006. In her second Games she became the first Paralympic curler ever to win gold twice in a row. In 2014 Gaudet set an even bigger record, winning gold for an incredible third time.

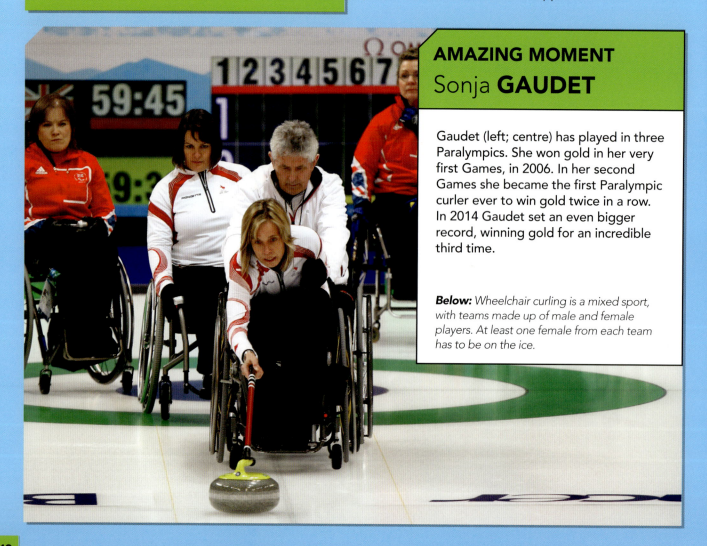

Below: Wheelchair curling is a mixed sport, with teams made up of male and female players. At least one female from each team has to be on the ice.

42

PARA ICE HOCKEY

Before 2016, para ice hockey was known as sledge hockey. Most of the rules are the same as for ice hockey. Games last three 15-minute periods. Each team can have up to 15 players, with six of them on the ice at any time. The sport is mixed, although almost all players are male. The biggest difference from Olympic ice hockey is the equipment. The players use special sledges fitted with two blades. They have two playing sticks, which they use to push themselves across the ice like a cross-country skier. The sticks are also used to control and shoot the puck.

Below: *Sweden (in yellow) take on Italy at para ice hockey at the 2018 Winter Olympics.*

BOBSLEIGH

In 2016, bobsleigh was added to the list of possible Winter Paralympic sports. The Paralympic organisers wanted to be sure the sport was popular enough before definitely including it for the 2022 Winter Paralympics.

"To compete at the Paralympic Games has been my dream since I started to play para ice hockey. It would be massive to be able to be there. But I want to deserve the place, not be awarded it."

– Norway's Lena Schrøder in 2017, hoping to become only the second female ice hockey player ever at the Paralympics. She was later chosen for Norway's 2018 Paralympic team.

43

SUPERSTARS EXTRA

The Paralympics has produced far too many superstar athletes to fit them all in a short book like this one. Here are just a few more Paralympic greats from the past and present:

Matt COWDREY

When he retired in 2015, Cowdrey was Australia's most successful Paralympic athlete. As well as 13 Paralympic titles he held five world records, five Paralympic records and had won 16 world-championship golds.

SPORT Swimming

3 13 7

PARALYMPIC MEDALS

Tanni GREY-THOMSON

Grey-Thomson's Paralympic wheelchair-racing career lasted 16 years. At distances between 100 metres and 800 metres she was almost unbeatable for much of that time. The medal haul began in 1988, when Grey-Thomson won a single bronze medal in the 400 metres. At her last Games, in 2004, she won gold medals number 10 and 11.

SPORT Track athletics

1 11 4

PARALYMPIC MEDALS

Libby KOSMALA

Kosmala is a legendary Australian Paralympian. She represented her country at 12 – yes, 12 – Games between 1972 and 2016. Her first ever medal was a bronze for swimming in 1972. After that, all the rest were for air-rifle shooting. Kosmala finally retired from Paralympic competition in 2016 after the London Paralympics, at the age of 74.

SPORT Air-rifle shooting, swimming

1 9 3

PARALYMPIC MEDALS

Left: Libby Kosmala

Ali **JAWAD**

Jawad was originally an international-level judo player, but switched to powerlifting. While still a teenager he was lifting some of the heaviest weights ever by British para powerlifters. Already a silver medallist at the 2016 Paralympics, Jawad aims to add gold to his collection in 2020.

0 0 1

PARALYMPIC MEDALS

Left: Ali Jawad

SPORT
Powerlifting

Ntando **MAHLANGU**

Imagine being in your first Paralympic Games at the age of 14 – that's what happened to Ntando Mahlangu. Not only that, he won a silver medal, just behind the defending champion, Great Britain's Richard Whitehead. If Mahlangu keeps improving at this speed, by the time he is fully grown he will be unbeatable.

0 0 1

PARALYMPIC MEDALS

SPORT
Track athletics

David **WEIR**

Powerhouse wheelchair racer David Weir is one of Great Britain's best-known Paralympians. As well as winning four golds at his home Games, the London 2012 Paralympics, he has won the London Marathon eight times.

1 6 1

PARALYMPIC MEDALS

SPORT
Track athletics

Trischa **ZORN**

Trischa Zorn is the most successful Paralympian ever. She is the only athlete who has won more medals at a Paralympic Games than Ragnhild Myklebust (see below). Zorn is a blind swimmer so good that in 1980 she missed out on qualifying for the US Olympic team by just hundredths of a second. At the Paralympics she raced at seven Games and was almost unbeatable.

5 41 9

PARALYMPIC MEDALS

Left: Trischa Zorn's last Paralympics were in 2004, when she won a bronze medal at the age of 40.

SPORT
Swimming

Ragnhild **MYKLEBUST**

No one yet has won more medals at a Winter Paralympics than Ragnhild Myklebust. It seems unlikely that anyone will ever beat her incredible record. As a cross-country skier she was unbeatable: from her first race at the 1972 Paralympics to her last in 2002, Myklebust never lost and collected 16 golds.

2 22 3

PARALYMPIC MEDALS

SPORT
Cross-country skiing, biathlon, ice-sledge speed racing

GLOSSARY & FIND OUT MORE

amputated cut off. People sometimes have to have part of their body amputated because it has been damaged or has not grown properly

blade in rowing and canoeing, a blade is the wide, flat end part of the paddle

blocks in swimming, the blocks (short for 'starting blocks') are a small, raised platform at the end of the pool, which athletes dive from

capsize turn over: a boat that capsizes tips up and goes upside-down in the water

cerebral palsy a neurological condition which makes the muscles weaker than normal

conservation preventing waste and pollution, particularly of things such as land, animal habitats, water and air

coordination ability to control the movement of your limbs

cox person who controls a rowing crew, giving them advice on steering and speed

disqualified removed from competition, so that your times and places are not counted in the final result

endurance ability to do something for a long time

grapple in judo and wrestling, grappling is when the fighters try to get a powerful grip on their opponent, then throw them

hand bike bicycle that is powered by pedals driven with the rider's hands, instead of their feet

host person or place that organises an event that other people are invited to. In the Paralympics the 'host' country is the one where the Games are held

ice-sledge hockey old name for the sport now called para ice hockey

impairment physical or mental condition that stop a person from doing something, or stops them doing it as well as they would be able to without the impairment

MBE Member of the British Empire, an award given to leading citizens of the UK and Commonwealth

medevac short for medical evacuation

medley in swimming, a medley is a race featuring three or four strokes. Medleys can have the same swimmer doing all the strokes or be team races, where each person does one of them

OBE Order of the British Empire, an award given to leading citizens of the UK and Commonwealth

offside rule rule in football that says the ball cannot be passed to a player who is ahead of the last defender

out of play off the field of play, for example when a football is kicked off the pitch

outfield player football player who is not the goalkeeper

outrigger small, streamlined float attached to the side of a boat to make it less likely to capsize

paraplegic unable to move your legs or lower body

physio short for physiotherapy, a way of treating physical problems using, for example, massage and heat instead of drugs

piste in fencing, the piste is the long, thin playing area

prosthetic limb artificial arm, leg or part of these limbs (such as the hand)

psyching out disturbing your opponent's concentration, so that they will not be able to perform as well

puck small hard disc used in para ice hockey

qualifying allowed or admitted. Someone in a wheelchair, for example, qualifies to play wheelchair basketball

reach distance your arm will stretch away from your body

rehabilitation recovery from an injury

tandem bicycle that can be ridden by two people

thought experiment experiment that is done in your mind, using your imagination, instead of in real life

tie-break contest to decide the winner of a game that is a draw

trunk (sometimes called the torso) the part of a person to which their neck, arms and legs are attached

veteran someone who fought in a war

weight division in boxing and other martial arts. Fighters are put into groups according to how much they weigh. These groups are called weight divisions

BOOKS TO READ
The Paralympics Nick Hunter (Wayland, 2012)
Unsinkable: From Russian Orphan to Paralympic Swimming World Champion Jessica Long with Hannah Long (HMH Books for Young Readers, 2018)
Paralympic Sports: Events Robin Johnson (Crabtree, 2009)

WEBSITES
The official Paralympics website is at ***paralympic. org***. The site is full of information about Paralympic events and competitors. On many of the pages about Summer Paralympic sports, there are links to videos explaining the key features. You can also click on a 'Ones to watch' tile to keep up to date with some of the athletes to look out for.

The organisers of the Tokyo 2020 Paralympics have put together an excellent site with up-to-date information about each sport. Find it at ***tokyo2020.org/en/games/sport/paralympic/***

NOTE TO PARENTS AND TEACHERS
Every effort has been made by the publisher to ensure that these websites contain no inappropriate or offensive material. However, because of the nature of the Internet, it is impossible to guarantee that the content of these sites will not be altered. We strongly advise that Internet access is supervised by a responsible adult.

INDEX

Altunoluk, Sevda 23
archery 5, 8, 29
athletics 4–6, 10–12, 18, 29, 44–45

badminton 5, 14
basketball, wheelchair 5–6, 29
biathlon 5, 40, 45
bobsleigh 42–43
boccia 4–5, 15

callers 12
canoeing 5, 16
classifications, Paralympic 6–7
Cowdrey, Matt 4, 44
curling, wheelchair 5, 15, 42
cycling 5–6, 18–19

equestrian 5–6

fencing, wheelchair 5, 36
football, five-a-side blind 4–5, 20–22

Gaudet, Sonja 42
goalball 5–7, 15, 22–23
Grey-Thomson, Tanni 44
guides 12–13, 41

handcycling 7, 18
history, Paralympics 5
hockey, ice 5, 42–43
Hollermann, Rose 29
Huckaby, Brenna 39

International Paralympic Committee 6

Jawad, Ali 45
Johnson, Michael 9
judo 5, 24, 45
jumps, long/high 4, 10

Kosmala, Libby 44

Lijing, Wang 24

McGrath, Curtis 16
McKeever, Brian 41
Mahlangu, Ntando 45

Morelli, Shawn 19
Moreno, Leomon 23
Myklebust, Ragnhild 45

Partyka, Natalia 34
Pascoe, Sophie 31
pictograms 5
powerlifting 5, 26–27, 45

racing, wheelchair 10, 44–45
Rahman, Siamand 27
Ricardinho 21
rowing 5, 17
rugby, wheelchair 5, 37
running 11–12

shooting 5, 7, 9, 40, 44
Simmonds, Ellie 33
skiing,
    alpine 5
    cross-country 5, 29, 40–41, 45
snowboarding 5, 38–39
swimming 4–6, 16, 18, 29–33, 44–45

table tennis 5, 34
taekwondo 5, 25
Tákacs, Károly 5
Takakuwa, Saki 4
tennis, wheelchair 5, 29, 35
triathlon 5, 13

Vio, Beatrice 36
volleyball, sitting 5, 28
Vongsa, Watcharahon 15

Weir, David 45
Wheelchair Games 5
Whitehead, Richard 11, 45

Zanardi, Alex 7
Zorn, Trischia 45